YOU CHOOSE BOOKS™

The
Japanese American
Internment

An Interactive History Adventure

by Rachael Hanel

Consultant:

Gina Wenger, PhD, Associate Professor of Art Education
Minnesota State University, Mankato
Author, "Documentary Photography:
Three Photographers' Standpoints on the
Japanese-American Internment"

Capstone
press®

Mankato, Minnesota

You Choose Books are published by Capstone Press,
151 Good Counsel Drive, P.O. Box 669, Mankato, Minnesota 56002.
www.capstonepress.com

Library of Congress Cataloging-in-Publication Data
Hanel, Rachael.
    The Japanese American internment : an interactive history adventure / by Rachael Hanel.
    p. cm. — (You choose books)
    Summary: "Describes the events surrounding the internment of Japanese Americans in relocation
centers during World War II. The reader's choices reveal the historical details from the perspective of
Japanese internees and Caucasians" — Provided by publisher.
    Includes bibliographical references and index.
    ISBN-13: 978-1-4296-1358-3 (hardcover)   ISBN-13: 978-1-4296-1765-9 (softcover pbk.)
    ISBN-10: 1-4296-1358-0 (hardcover)   ISBN-10: 1-4296-1765-9 (softcover pbk.)
    1. Japanese Americans — Evacuation and relocation, 1942–1945. 2. World War, 1939–1945 —
Japanese Americans. 3. World War, 1939–1945 — Personal narratives, American. I. Title. II. Series.
D769.8.A6H35 2008
940.54'8252 — dc22   2007034232

Editorial Credits
Megan Schoeneberger, editor; Juliette Peters, set designer; Gene Bentdahl, book designer;
    Wanda Winch, photo researcher; Danielle Ceminsky, illustrator

Photo Credits
AP Images, 6; Archie Miyatake, from the Toyo Miyatake Manzanar Collection, cover; The Bancroft
Library, University of California, Berkeley, 1967.014 v.18-BE-149--PIC, 20; The Bancroft Library,
University of California, Berkeley, 1967.014 v.19 CB-8--PIC, 29; The Bancroft Library, University of
California, Berkeley, 1967.014 v.26 CD-307--PIC, 90; The Bancroft Library, University of California,
Berkeley, 1967.014 v.26 DE-312--PIC, 72; The Bancroft Library, University of California, Berkeley,
1967.014 v.26 DE-348--PIC, 79; The Bancroft Library, University of California, Berkeley, 1967.014
v.26 DE-364--PIC, 95; The Bancroft Library, University of California, Berkeley, 1967.014 v.28 DH-
493--PIC, 83; The Bancroft Library, University of California, Berkeley, 1967.014 v.66 HG-571-PIC,
52; The Bancroft Library, University of California, Berkeley, 1967.014 v.78 B-470--PIC, 56; California
State Archives, 60; Charles E. Young Research Library, UCLA, Department of Special Collections, Los
Angeles Daily News Photographic Archives, Negative Collection, Members of the Japanese American
Citizens' League, ca. 1941, uclamss_1387_b51_27053, 19; Corbis, 98; Corbis/Bettmann, 9, 36, 81, 103;
Corbis/Russell Lee, 100; Getty Images Inc./Hulton Archive, 14; Getty Images Inc./Time Life Pictures/
Al Fenn, 33; Gift of Bob and Rumi Uragami, Japanese American National Museum (93.179.2), 105; Gift
of Jack and Peggy Iwata, Japanese American National Museum (93.102.23), 17; Gift of Jack and Peggy
Iwata, Japanese American National Museum (93.102.42), 65; Gift of Jack and Peggy Iwata, Japanese
American National Museum (93.102.7), 66; Gift of Jack and Peggy Iwata, Japanese American National
Museum (93.102.80), 58; Library of Congress, 16, 26, 42; National Japanese American Historical
Society, 12; Special Collections Dept., J. Willard Marriott Library, University of Utah, 44, 46; University
of Southern California, Doheny Memorial Library, Specialized Libraries and Archival Collections, 68

1 2 3 4 5 6 13 12 11 10 09 08

TABLE OF CONTENTS

ABOUT YOUR ADVENTURE

YOU are living in the United States when the Japanese attack Pearl Harbor. As the country prepares for war, some people are uneasy about the Japanese living among them. How do you respond?

In this book, you'll explore how the choices people made affected their lives. The events you'll experience happened to real people.

Chapter One sets the scene. Then you choose which path to read. Follow the directions at the bottom of each page. The choices you make will change your outcome. After you finish one path, go back and read the others for new perspectives and more adventures.

YOU CHOOSE the path
you take through history.

The Japanese attack on Pearl Harbor destroyed American ships and airplanes.

A Day of Infamy

For more than two years, war has spread through Europe like wildfire. It started when Germany attacked Poland in September 1939. The United Kingdom, France, and other countries declared war on Germany. Fighting spread to Italy, Greece, northern Africa, and the Soviet Union. Somehow, the United States stayed out of it — until now. Japan has brought war to America's doorstep.

Yesterday morning, Japanese planes bombed American ships and planes at the Pearl Harbor military base in Hawaii. The surprise attack killed more than 2,300 Americans.

Turn the page.

Now, like millions of other Americans, you turn on the radio to hear the president. "Yesterday, December 7, 1941 — a date which will live in infamy — the United States of America was suddenly and deliberately attacked by naval and air forces of the Empire of Japan," U.S. President Franklin Delano Roosevelt begins.

The president asks Congress to declare war on Japan. A few hours later, Canada and the United Kingdom join the United States. In a few days, Germany and Italy declare war on the United States. World War II becomes a truly global war.

Americans fear another attack. Could the West Coast be next on the Japanese military's list? A large number of Japanese Americans live in California, Oregon, and Washington. Could they be spies? Could they be plotting with the enemy back in Japan?

After the attack on Pearl Harbor, Japanese Americans became the victims of discrimination.

Thousands of Japanese people live in the United States. Most of them are American citizens. The Nisei, as they call themselves, were born here. But according to law, their parents and any others who came directly from Japan are not allowed to become citizens. They are known as the Issei.

Turn the page.

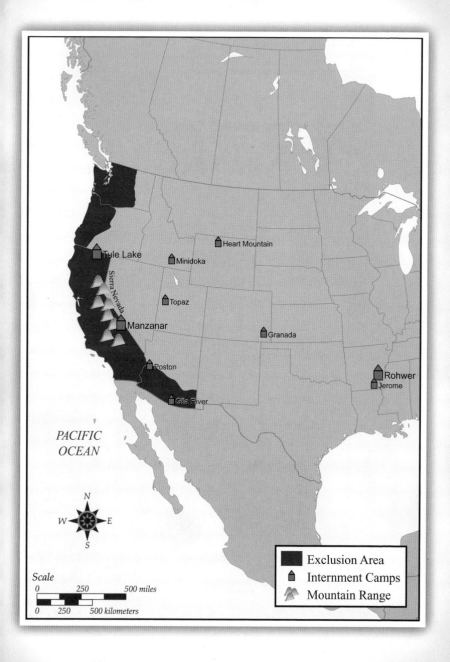

Heart Mountain

Tule Lake

Minidoka

Sierra Nevada

Topaz

Manzanar

Granada

Poston

Rohwer
Jerome

Gila River

PACIFIC
OCEAN

N
W — E
S

Exclusion Area
Internment Camps
Mountain Range

Scale
0   250   500 miles
0   250   500 kilometers

On February 19, 1942, President Roosevelt signs Executive Order 9066. All people of Japanese ancestry living on the West Coast will be removed from their homes. They will be placed in 10 War Relocation Authority (WRA) camps. That way, the government can watch what the Japanese Americans say and do.

Camp life is different for each person. Everyone faces many decisions. Each person's experience in camp will depend on the choices they make.

➤ To go to the Manzanar camp in southern California, turn to page **13**.

➤ To go to the Tule Lake camp in northern California, turn to page **43**.

➤ To be a teacher in the Rohwer camp in Arkansas, turn to page **73**.

Soldiers delivered evacuation notices to Japanese Americans who lived on the West Coast.

CHAPTER 2

Behind Barbed Wire

You have just one week to get ready for evacuation. "We can't just leave the grocery store," your mother worries. "Who will run it?"

"We'll have to sell it," your father says. He finds a man willing to pay $400 cash for the store and everything in it. The business is worth much more, but your father can't wait for a better offer. "Four hundred bucks is better than nothing," he says.

On March 30, 1942, an army truck takes your family to the train station. The train takes you to the Manzanar camp in southern California.

Turn the page.

You get off the train, stretch, and look around Manzanar. Dust swirls in the dry desert air. The Sierra Nevada mountain range rises in the distance. Eight guard towers anchor the corners of the camp. Men with guns patrol the grounds.

Hot desert winds coated the Manzanar camp with dust.

Row after row of barracks line the dirt streets. Tar paper covers the wooden buildings. There are 36 blocks, with 14 barracks in each block. Each barrack contains four apartments.

Your family's apartment is a small single room. The walls don't go all the way to the ceiling. You can hear people talking and a baby crying next door. There are no chairs or tables in the apartment, only beds.

"Where is the bathroom?" you ask.

"Showers and toilets are in another building," your father answers. "Everyone shares."

Even meals are shared. Everyone eats together in the mess hall. At first, your family sits together. But after a few weeks, you sit with some other kids your age. You quickly become friends with your neighbor, James Ito.

Turn the page.

Job offers for internees were posted on the Help Wanted board at Manzanar.

After a few months, the two of you decide to get jobs. You go to the administration building to see what's available. "I have a couple of choices for you," a man says. "You can work in the mess hall. Or you could harvest sugar beets in Idaho."

You think for a moment. Harvesting sugar beets would be hard work, harder than the kitchen job. But it would allow you to leave camp for a few months.

→ To work in the camp kitchen, go to page **17**.

→ To work on the farm, turn to page **20**.

You and James take the jobs in the mess hall. You get up at 5:00 each morning to go to work. You and other kitchen workers make and serve breakfast and lunch. Your shift ends after lunch is served. You spend afternoons playing baseball with your friends.

Mess halls in each camp provided jobs for many internees.

Turn the page.

As weeks pass, you and the other workers notice supplies are missing. The same amount of food is trucked into the camp each week. But suddenly you have barely enough ingredients to make soy sauce. Harry Ueno, the head of the kitchen workers' union, investigates. He learns that camp officials are taking food and selling it to people outside the camp.

On December 5, 1942, Ueno is arrested. Camp officials say it's because he's suspected of beating up a fellow internee, Fred Tayama. But your fellow kitchen workers don't believe it.

"It's just a cover-up," James says to you. "Ueno was really arrested because he accused officials of stealing our food." A meeting is planned for that evening at the main administration building.

"I don't think you should join that meeting," your mother says. "The guards have guns. You could be arrested or killed."

"I'm going," James says. You see hundreds of people walking that way. "Are you coming?"

Fred Tayama was attacked in his Manzanar apartment on December 5, 1942.

➤ To stay at your apartment, turn to page **22**.

➤ To join the crowd, turn to page **23**.

James decides to work in the mess hall, but you choose to work at the sugar beet farm. Day after day, you stoop low to cut the beets out of the ground. Your back and arms ache. The farmer constantly barks orders at you and your fellow workers.

Due to a shortage of workers, farmers hired men from the internment camps to help harvest crops.

You return to Manzanar in early 1943. "Where's James?" you ask your mother.

Your mother motions for you to sit down. "I have bad news," she says. She explains that Harry Ueno, one of the kitchen workers, accused camp officials of taking food meant for internees. "They put Harry in jail. They said Harry had beaten up another man. But the kitchen workers said it was a cover-up."

"What happened?"

"A big riot broke out to free Harry. In the end, the military fired on the crowd. Two people were killed."

"And James?" you ask.

"Your friend James was one of them."

Turn to page **25**.

"No, I'm not coming," you tell James. "I'm going to stay here with my parents."

"I'll tell you all about it later," James says.

After an hour or so, you hear shouts coming from the administration and police buildings. Then, you hear gunshots.

"Oh my, what was that?" your mother asks, worried.

You peek your head out the door. Dozens of people are running toward the administration building.

"I'm going to see what's going on," you yell as you run out of the apartment.

Turn to page 24.

You join a group of about 500 men who march to the camp jail. The goal is to free Harry. Soon, military police arrive with their guns. The crowd chants and sings. Some men yell loudly. The soldiers look nervous. Then, you hear gunshots.

Turn the page.

You run toward the administration building. Several internees lie on the ground. Some are moaning and bleeding, while others don't move at all.

You search for James. You notice a small crowd has gathered around one of the victims. You shove your way to the front in time to see James being carried to the hospital. Blood spills from his chest and stomach.

At the hospital, James is pronounced dead. A few days later, another man, Jim Kanagawa, dies from his injuries.

You are in shock. James was only 17. How could he be dead? You're afraid to do or say anything that might anger the camp officials.

In February 1943, the WRA hands out a questionnaire to everyone age 17 and older at all 10 camps. You easily answer questions about relatives in the United States and in Japan. But questions 27 and 28 are difficult. Question 27 asks if you are willing to join the U.S. armed forces. Question 28 asks you to swear loyalty to the United States and deny allegiance to the Japanese emperor.

"What should I say?" you ask your parents.

Turn the page.

Families were afraid of being split up based on their answers to the loyalty questionnaire.

"It's good to appear loyal. Look at what happened when Harry Ueno caused trouble," your mother says.

"Your mother and I aren't U.S. citizens," your father says. "What if we are sent back to Japan when all of this is over? If we answer yes and deny loyalty to the emperor, we could be jailed or even killed."

"But I won't answer yes if you answer no," you say. "You never know what the government might do. We could be split up."

Your mother agrees. "We should probably answer the questions in the same way, so at least we have a better chance of staying together."

You don't have much time to decide. The camp officials demand an answer.

➻ To answer yes to both questions and pledge allegiance to the United States, turn to page **30**.

➻ To answer no to both questions and remain loyal to Japan, turn to page **53**.

You and your parents decide to answer yes. Soon, you find out that most other internees at Tule Lake answered no. Officials have decided to bring everybody who answered no from other camps to Tule Lake. To make room for them, internees who answered yes are sent to other camps.

You and your parents arrive by train at Manzanar in southern California. The camp sits at the foot of the Sierra Nevada mountain range. The view is a welcome change from Tule Lake. But the rest of the camp is familiar. It has the same barracks, mess halls, and recreation centers as Tule Lake.

After arriving in Manzanar, internees hauled their belongings to their barracks.

Your new neighbor, Tom, is a young man about your age. You tell him about Tule Lake, and he tells you about Manzanar. You learn that there was a riot a couple of months ago. Two young men were killed.

Turn to page 31.

You answer yes to both questions. You soon learn that all people who answered no are being sent to the Tule Lake camp in northern California.

The few people from Tule Lake who answered yes are sent to other camps. You meet Tom, a young man from Tule Lake who is assigned to the kitchen crew. "People at Tule Lake are quite nervous now," he tells you. "Nobody knows what will happen next."

Sometimes, you and Tom talk about leaving the camp for good. You're not sure how much more of this camp life you can take.

"The army is creating an all-Nisei unit. I'm going to join," Tom says. "How about you?"

"I've been thinking about college," you say. Last week, members of the National Japanese American Student Relocation Council visited the camp. They offered to help students apply to colleges.

The process for getting admitted while you're in camp is quite slow. Joining the army would get you out of the camp right away. But that choice could also get you killed.

➤ *To apply for college, turn to page* **32**.

➤ *To join the army, turn to page* **33**.

You don't feel right fighting for a country that has taken away your freedom. "I'm going to college," you say.

Your first school of choice is the University of Colorado. But after waiting several weeks, you receive a letter from the university. They refuse to accept any Japanese American students.

You are discouraged. But the counselor at the National Japanese American Student Relocation Council suggests applying to the University of Texas in Austin, Texas. Other Japanese students have already been accepted there. Should you try again? Or maybe there's still time to join the army.

➤ To join the army, turn to page **35**.

➤ To apply to the University of Texas, turn to page **37**.

Japanese American soldiers trained at Camp Shelby in Mississippi.

If the government thinks you are disloyal, joining the military will prove them wrong. You become part of the 442nd Regimental Combat Team, an all-Nisei unit. At Camp Shelby, Mississippi, you meet the 100th Battalion, a unit made up of Japanese American men from Hawaii. In 1944, the two units combine to form the 442nd Regimental Combat Team/100th Battalion.

Turn the page.

One day, an officer approaches you and your fellow soldiers. "We need Japanese translators in the Pacific," he says. "Soldiers who know the Japanese language can help us crack codes and win the war." Volunteers would go to Fort Snelling in Minnesota for language training.

You think it over. You already know Japanese, and your skills would be valuable. But you've trained for battle with your fellow soldiers. You feel close to them and don't want to leave them.

➤ *To stay with your unit and fight,*
turn to page **39**.

➤ *To go to Fort Snelling for language training,*
turn to page **40**.

The University of Texas accepts your application. But you can't leave yet. The government must approve the school you have chosen. You also must apply for clearance to leave the camp.

You finally receive a letter from the student relocation council. "Get ready for Texas," it says. The council has sent your documents to Washington. Your permit should arrive in about 10 days.

Near the end of January 1944, you leave for Texas. Your mother is worried. "When the neighbor's daughter went to college, people called her horrible names, like 'Jap,'" she says.

You hate that word. It is said with prejudice and contempt. It may sound innocent, but it is meant to hurt.

Turn the page.

But the people in Texas are kind. They treat you just like any other student.

In college, you take science classes. You decide that you would like to be a doctor. The classes are challenging, but you work hard and are a good student. You want your parents to be proud.

You graduate and move on to medical school in Chicago. When the war ends, your family joins you. Your father takes a job at a small grocery store. You're all happy to be together again and glad that your camp experience is over.

THE END

To follow another path, turn to page 11.
To read the conclusion, turn to page 101.

In October 1944, you're sent to the Vosges Mountains in northeastern France. Your unit must rescue the Lost Battalion, 200 Texas soldiers trapped by 6,000 Germans.

After six days, you reach the soldiers. Many of them are dead. You help carry wounded soldiers down the hill. Bullets whiz past as you struggle under the weight of the wounded soldier.

Suddenly, there is a sharp pain in your stomach. You look down and see blood. As you drop to the ground, you think of your parents and picture their faces. It's the last thought you have. You become one of the 54 men who die rescuing the Lost Battalion.

THE END

To follow another path, turn to page 11.
To read the conclusion, turn to page 101.

The Military Intelligence Service Language School is the military's only Japanese language training school. As a student, you practice reading, writing, and speaking the Japanese language. Other classes teach code breaking, map reading, and radio monitoring.

After graduation, you're sent to the Philippine Islands in the Pacific Ocean. A few army leaders distrust Japanese American soldiers. They don't think you should be sent to the Pacific. But they soon realize how valuable you can be.

Japanese soldiers talk to each other in codes that you pick up on radio airwaves. Because of your training, you break their codes. The U.S. military now knows where the Japanese plan to attack next. The United States stays one step ahead of the Japanese and defeats them in 1945. You return home to the United States a hero.

THE END

To follow another path, turn to page 11.
To read the conclusion, turn to page 101.

Internees could bring only as much as they could carry to the camps.

CHAPTER 3

A Camp Apart

Your family has just received notice to evacuate next week. The U.S. government is making you leave your home, your school, and your friends. Even the family dog must be left behind.

May 15, 1942, is evacuation day. You and your family walk four blocks to the bus stop. You each carry one suitcase packed with clothing, bedding, and other necessary items. Armed soldiers herd you onto the bus.

At the Puyallup Fairgrounds in Washington, your family is assigned to a room under the grandstand. All six of you share a space that used to be a horse stall.

Turn the page.

"We won't be here long," your father says. "Just until they finish building the camps."

"*Shikata ga nai*," your mother says in Japanese. "It cannot be helped."

After a few months, you are moved to Tule Lake in northern California. The air here is hot and dry. Dirt and sand fly into your eyes. Barbed wire fences and guard towers surround the camp.

The Tule Lake camp consisted of rows of housing called barracks.

The outside of your building is covered with thin black tar paper. Your apartment is small and cramped, only 20 feet by 20 feet.

There is no furniture in the room except for cots. You find scrap lumber and build tables and chairs. Your mother sews curtains and cushions. But this room still doesn't feel like a home.

You've just finished high school and are old enough to get a job. The camp has a hospital, a blacksmith shop, a shoe repair shop, a cafeteria, and even a farm.

"A carpenter earns $19 a month plus a clothing allowance," the camp official tells you. "Or, you could work in the hospital. That job pays $16 a month, but it's indoors."

➤ To work as a carpenter, turn to page **46**.
➤ To work as a hospital orderly, turn to page **48**.

Internees were not allowed to leave the camps without permission.

You decide to take the carpentry job. You do odd jobs around camp, pounding nails into anything that needs to be fixed. You work every day of the week except Sunday. The work is hard, but when you're busy, time passes quickly.

You look for fun activities to do in your spare time. One day, you and several friends get permission to leave camp. You hike up to Castle Rock in the hills above the camp.

"It's really pretty up here, isn't it?" your friend says. "It's a shame that we have to go back," you say. "Wouldn't it be nice to just walk away?"

Everyone agrees, but escaping the camp isn't a serious choice. Where would you go if you succeeded? You wouldn't be able to blend in on the outside. Anyone who saw you would report you, and you'd be caught. Who knows what would happen when you came back? You could get into trouble, or even be beaten. Feeling helpless, you walk back to camp.

Turn to page 49.

The weather is so hot at Tule Lake. You decide to take a job that lets you work indoors, even if the pay is a little less.

You clean medical instruments, mop floors, and help move patients. You are shocked by the lack of supplies. There are not enough linens, pillows, or bedpans for all of the patients. The electricity often goes out. But the doctors are trained well, and they do the best they can with what they have.

By February 1943, many people are leaving the camps to find work, join the military, or go to college. The government wants to make sure their loyalty can be trusted. So the WRA passes out a questionnaire.

All internees age 17 and older at all 10 WRA camps must answer the questions. You answer questions about your savings, what magazines and newspapers you read, and your hobbies. But two questions in particular are tough to answer. Question 27 asks if you are "willing to serve in the armed forces of the United States in combat duty." And Question 28 asks if you will swear allegiance to the United States and "foreswear any form of allegiance or obedience to the Japanese emperor." You discuss these questions with your parents.

Turn the page.

"We're not sure how to answer," your father says. "We were never allowed to become U.S. citizens. If we answer no, we'll appear to be disloyal to the United States. Who knows what will happen to us?"

"But what if we're sent back to Japan after the war?" your mother says. "If we answer yes, people might find out we gave up our loyalty to Japan and the emperor. We could be thrown in jail or even killed!"

You are an American citizen. But you could be sent to Japan at any time. You're not sure how much loyalty you feel toward a country that keeps you locked up.

"And if I answer yes," you say, "and you answer no, what would happen then?"

Your father nods. "We should answer all the questions the same way. That way, no matter what happens, at least we'll be together."

You and your family must make a decision.

✦ *To answer yes to both questions, turn to page **28**.*

✦ *To answer no to both questions, turn to page **52**.*

People who answered no to the loyalty questionnaire were sent to Tule Lake.

You're not alone in answering no. More internees at Tule Lake answer no to the loyalty questions than at any other camp. For that reason, WRA officials decide to make Tule Lake a segregated camp. Those who answered no to the questions at other camps will be sent here, while those answering yes at Tule Lake will be sent to other camps.

You watch as trains bring in new internees. Pretty soon, you have new neighbors.

Turn to page 54.

You and your parents answer no to the questions. You soon find out that everyone who answered no will be sent to the Tule Lake camp in northern California. That way, the government can keep all the "disloyals" together.

For the second time in just a few months, you find yourself on a hot, stuffy train. At Tule Lake, the air is dry and dusty, just like it was in Manzanar.

You wonder what kind of trouble might happen here. It's clear that most internees at Tule Lake are willing to speak out against the government. You can feel the tension rising.

Turn the page.

One night, the family next door invites your family over to their apartment. You all talk about life in the camps.

"The government's treatment is terrible and unjust," says your neighbor. "We live behind barbed wire. Guards in the towers hold rifles. There isn't always enough food. Our toilets are in one open room. The showers are that way too. We don't have any privacy."

"It's shameful," you agree.

"Several of us are forming a resistance group called Sokoku Kenkyu Seinen Dan. Camp officials need to know how upset we are."

"I don't know how much good that will do," your mother says. "The government is so big. It would be hard to change their minds."

"What about you?" Your neighbor turns to you. "Our group could use some young people like you."

"Our only hope is to try to change things. If we stay quiet, nothing will change," you say. "Perhaps if we work together, we can get them to improve the conditions here."

"That's great," says your neighbor. "You would make a good block leader. You listen to all the people in the block and share their concerns at our meetings. Or we need teachers and military drill instructors for our Japanese language schools."

Which do you choose?

→ To become a block leader, turn to page **56**.

→ To help out in the schools, turn to page **58**.

As a block leader, you attend meetings with leaders of other blocks. You also join the committee that meets with camp officials. But Raymond Best, the camp director, refuses to make any changes.

Dillon Myer, shown here with First Lady Eleanor Roosevelt, was in charge of the War Relocation Authority.

Dillon Myer, the national WRA director, visits in November 1943. The committee meets with him. You tell him there is not enough food for everyone. "Mr. Myer, please listen to us," you say. "People are being treated like animals in cages. Can you improve the camp conditions?"

"I trust Mr. Best," Myer says. "He's in charge. It's up to him whether he wants to change things here."

You're angry that Myer won't help you. After the meeting, you report to the thousands of internees who have gathered outside. The crowd boos at your news. You see anger on everyone's faces.

Turn to page **60.**

Some students attended Japanese-language schools in Tule Lake.

"Japanese children need to know about their ancestry," you say. "I would like to help in the Japanese schools."

The camp officials know about the Japanese schools, but they don't try to shut them down. If they did, there would be angry protests. Most of the Japanese schools last only half a school day. During the other half, the children attend American schools.

In your free time, you join the Sokoku Kenkyu Seinen Dan. The men in this pro-Japan group hold military exercises and follow Japanese customs.

In late October 1943, the national director of the camps, Dillon Myer, visits Tule Lake. The block leaders meet with him to discuss camp conditions. "We should go to the administration building," your father says. "I want to know how the meeting went."

There's a large crowd at the administration building. After a few hours, the leaders come out. "There will be no changes. Myer dismissed the committee's concerns," they report. You boo, hiss, and stamp your feet. All around you, people are furious.

Turn the page.

To your surprise, there's no violence. But the large, noisy crowd makes the officials nervous. They fear a riot could happen in the future. For that reason, the camp director calls upon the army to put Tule Lake under martial law.

After the protest, news of the event was reported in local newspapers.

For the next two months, troops patrol the camp with loaded guns. Tanks roll through camp, and barbed wire fences are placed between the barracks and the administration buildings. When Best decides the threat has passed, martial law ends.

On July 1, 1944, President Roosevelt signs Public Law 405. This law allows internees to give up their American citizenship.

"What should I do now?" you think. You wonder what will happen if you give up your citizenship. Will you be sent back to Japan? You don't know whether to stick to your beliefs and answer yes, or play it safe and answer no.

➤ *To give up your citizenship, turn to page **62**.*

➤ *To stay a U.S. citizen, turn to page **65**.*

It might be best to go back to Japan after the war. That will be easier to do if you are not a U.S. citizen. You are one of 5,461 internees at Tule Lake who give up their citizenship.

A few days later, you hear a sharp knock at your door. You open the door and see camp policemen. "You're a member of the Sokoku Kenkyu Seinen Dan, aren't you?"

You nod.

"Come with us. All resistance members are a threat."

The policemen declare you to be pro-Japan and anti-American. They say you are an enemy of the United States. After a few days in the Tule Lake jail, you are sent to a Department of Justice prison camp in North Dakota.

Fort Lincoln in Bismarck, North Dakota, is a prison. The only exercise you get is walking back and forth between your small cell and the cafeteria.

Turn the page.

On August 6, 1945, the United States drops an atomic bomb on the Japanese city of Hiroshima. Three days later, the United States drops a second atomic bomb on the Japanese city of Nagasaki. Both of the cities are destroyed. More than 100,000 people die.

On August 14, Japan agrees to end the war. They officially surrender on September 2, and World War II finally ends.

You had planned to move to Japan after the war. But the country faces a long recovery. The government is unstable, and the economy is weak. What kind of life will you find there?

At the same time, if you stay in America, you won't be an American citizen. What choice will you make?

➤ *To move to Japan, turn to page* **68**.

➤ *To stay in America, turn to page* **70**.

Young musicians formed an orchestra at Tule Lake.

Deep in your heart, you know there are good things about America. After all, your parents chose this country so you could have a better life. You decide to keep your citizenship.

Instead of going to resistance meetings, you focus on making the best of what you have. Some young men form baseball teams, and you become a star pitcher. You attend dances and go to concerts performed by the Tule Lake Symphony.

Turn the page.

By December 1944, the U.S. Supreme Court rules that the government cannot hold loyal citizens against their will. Some internees leave. But if the government suspects a person is not loyal, that person must stay in camp. About 5,000 Tule Lake internees who are part of pro-Japan organizations have to stay.

Families were happy to receive their permit to move out of the camps.

The war ends in August 1945 when the United States drops atomic bombs on the Japanese cities of Hiroshima and Nagasaki. Your heart aches for people living there, but you're glad the war is over.

You're free to go home, but you're not sure where that is. The home you left behind is gone, sold because there was no way to make payments while in the camps. Across the country, many whites have not welcomed Japanese Americans into their communities. Maybe you should just move to Japan.

→ To move to Japan, turn to page **68**.

→ To stay in the United States, turn to page **71**.

Many internees chose to move to Japan after leaving the camps.

You've had enough of America and its camps. In December, you, your family, and about 1,300 other former Tule Lake internees board a ship to Japan. As the ship enters the Tokyo Harbor, you see the mountain known as Fujiyama in the distance. The sky is clear, and the view is breathtaking.

As soon as you step off the ship, you are herded onto a train. The train carries you to Hiroshima. There, you hope to find relatives.

In Hiroshima, nearly every building was destroyed or badly damaged. Countless people died the day the bomb was dropped. Tens of thousands more have died since that day.

You find your relatives living in a tiny metal shack. They were in a different city when the bomb fell. They lost everything, but at least they are alive.

You move into their crowded shack. When spring arrives, your family plants a vegetable garden around the shack. You all begin the long task of building a new life in Japan.

THE END

To follow another path, turn to page 11.
To read the conclusion, turn to page 101.

You stay in the United States. But you are not a U.S. citizen, because you signed that piece of paper. You cannot vote. You are considered an enemy alien.

You hear from other former internees who also gave up their American citizenship. You want your rights back. Lawyer Wayne Mortimer Collins agrees to fight on your behalf. He battles the Department of Justice for years. Collins argues that your decision to give up citizenship should not count because it was made under stress. Finally, Congress and President Richard Nixon restore your citizenship in 1971. You are an American again, 25 years after World War II ended.

THE END

To follow another path, turn to page 11.
To read the conclusion, turn to page 101.

While you were in camp, your home was sold to pay for debts. You and your parents must start over.

Your father struggles to find a job. Businesses don't want to hire Japanese men. Your father answers Help Wanted ads looking for gardeners. He works hard and soon has several customers.

Your family moves into a new house. Your neighbors welcome you. They share food from their gardens. They bring you clothes to wear. One gives you a job in his office.

Even with their help, years pass before you can live the way you did before the war. You hope that someday the government will apologize for your hardships.

THE END

To follow another path, turn to page 11.
To read the conclusion, turn to page 101.

Some of the earliest internees at Rohwer were put to work building housing for the camp staff.

CHAPTER 4

The Teacher's Story

All your life, you've lived in a small town in Arkansas. Few Japanese people live in the South. In fact, many Southerners have never met an Asian person.

In early 1942, the War Relocation Authority announces its plans to build two relocation camps in Arkansas. The camps will hold Japanese people forced out of their homes by the evacuation order on the West Coast. Governor Adkins allows it, but only after insisting that the Japanese be kept under guard.

Turn the page.

In early July, government workers begin building the camps. But the projects fall behind. When the first internees arrive in September, they are put to work.

In October, John Trice visits the high school where you are a teacher. Trice is the school superintendent at the Rohwer relocation camp near the town of McGehee. "We need teachers," he says.

He offers good wages — higher than what most teachers usually receive. But you'll be expected to live in the camp year-round.

➤ *To turn the job down, go to page 75.*

➤ *To accept the job, turn to page 76.*

You turn the job down. The camps, with their small barracks and barbed wire fences, look like prisons. You wouldn't feel comfortable living there.

"Good choice," another teacher tells you. "Those camp teachers will have a hard time finding a job around here after the war. Who wants to teach those Jap kids anyway?"

You hate when people use that word to talk about the internees. "These so-called Japs are people, not monsters. And many of them are American citizens. They deserve an education like everyone else." Maybe you should change your mind and take the job.

❧ To change your mind and take the job,
turn to page **76**.

❧ To keep your job at the local school,
turn to page **80**.

You decide to take the job. Maybe you can help improve the internees' experiences, even just a little.

You sign up to teach civics to high school students. A few weeks later, you pack your bags. Classes will begin in November.

While you pack, your aunt Cora calls. She lives in McGehee and wants you to visit. You haven't seen her for a while. But you have an appointment with the camp director. Do you have enough time?

❖ *To stop and see Aunt Cora, go to page* **77**.

❖ *To go directly to camp, turn to page* **79**.

Internees boarded trains at Santa Anita assembly center in California. The trains carried the internees to Rohwer in Arkansas.

Johnston leads you along a wooden sidewalk. You pass families just arriving from California. One woman holds a baby. An elderly man walks beside her with a cane. Several teenagers greet each other with hugs. Since being forced out of their homes, the internees have lived at temporary assembly centers in California. They've known each other for several months.

Turn the page.

The camp looks even more miserable than you expected. Thin black tar paper covers the outside of the army-style buildings. That's not going to shield the cold in winter or the hot winds in summer.

"It may not look like much," Johnston says. "But internees get three meals a day and a warm place to sleep. That's more than what many of the local people have."

Johnston stops in front of the staff barracks. He points to the end of a long row of buildings. "There's your classroom. You can check it out after you unpack. I've got a meeting to attend."

Your apartment is tiny. There's hardly room for the cot and an army stove. It doesn't take long to unpack. Then you head to your classroom.

Wooden sidewalks covered the wet, swampy ground at Rohwer.

As you walk to your classroom, you get a better view of the camp. There are more than 600 buildings in the camp. They are divided into 51 blocks surrounded by a barbed wire fence. Each block has 12 barracks, a mess hall, and a combined bathroom and laundry building. Eight guard towers overlook the camp.

Turn the page.

The school building looks just like all the other buildings in the camp. Your classroom has no desks, only a few benches and some tree stumps for chairs. There is no chalkboard. You don't see any pens, pencils, or any other supplies.

How are you supposed to teach without any supplies? It might take weeks before you receive any. Maybe you could go into McGehee and buy what you need.

✦ *To go to McGehee, go to page* **85**.

✦ *To make do until supplies arrive, turn to page* **86**.

In McGehee, you buy pens, pencils, and notebook paper for the students. You also pick up a copy of the Little Rock newspaper to read later. As you leave the store, a young man tips his hat. "Hello," he says. "You must be new to town." You chat with the man for a few minutes, and he invites you to dinner.

"I really need to get back to camp," you say. "Maybe some other time."

"You mean Rohwer?" he asks. "Aren't you afraid the Japanese are plotting something terrible? Honestly, I'm nervous to have that many living so close to this town."

"There's nothing to be scared of," you say. "Most of them are American citizens. The government is locking them up like enemies." Frustrated, you return to camp.

Turn the page.

When you wake up the next morning, your body aches from sleeping on the small, hard cot.

After breakfast in the mess hall, you return to your room to read the newspaper. One article complains that internees receive special treatment.

But you haven't seen any sign of internees receiving special treatment. They live in tiny apartments with hardly any privacy. They must share bathrooms, showers, and laundry areas.

You decide to write a letter to the newspaper. You want people to know the truth.

You're about to put the letter in an envelope when there's a knock at the door. It's Miss Avery, one of the other teachers. You ask her if she wants to put her name on the letter too.

"I agree with you," she says. "But I don't think it's a good idea to stir up trouble so early in our jobs here. Mr. Johnston might get mad if there's a letter in the newspaper. You don't want to take the chance of losing your job, do you?"

→ *To wait, turn to page **88**.*

→ *To send the letter, turn to page **89**.*

Instead of mailing the letter, you set it aside for another day. Maybe in a few months, you might feel more comfortable sending it. You're new here, and you don't want to cause trouble.

"I think it's best to wait," Miss Avery says. "Maybe we could get everyone together, and we could write a letter to the editor as a group. That way, not just one of us is singled out. As a group, they might take us more seriously."

"That's a good idea," you say. "Let's keep that in mind."

*Turn to page **90**.*

You send the letter anyway. A few days later, your letter appears in the town newspaper. That afternoon, Mr. Johnston talks to you.

"I saw your letter," he says. "We're not exactly welcome here by the locals. We should be careful not to stir up any trouble. I urge you not to do something like that again. I like you, but my bosses don't want anyone here who's going to rock the boat."

You nod. Even though Mr. Johnston was upset, you still think sending the letter was the right thing to do.

Turn the page.

Classrooms at Rohwer were bare and lacked basic supplies such as desks for each student.

Classes begin the next day. You and the students make do with the benches and tree stumps. Eventually, some real desks arrive, as do the textbooks. Over the next few months, you and the students settle into your daily schedules. In addition to your civics class, they study English, science, math, art, and music.

In early February, you give a lesson on democracy. "Democracy means a government that goes by the will of the people," you explain.

"Then why don't we get a say in how the government treats us?" one young man asks. "Many races and religious groups make up the United States. A democracy should go by the will of *all* its people."

The other students shout in agreement. "The government keeps us here against our will," says another student. "Does this look like democracy to you?"

"I understand," you say. "But a democracy isn't always fair."

The students boo you. Some slam their books shut and walk out. You dismiss the class for the day.

Turn the page.

The next day, the students apologize for their behavior. "We got so upset because of the loyalty questionnaire," one girl explains. A few days ago, the WRA gave this list of questions to everyone age 17 or older. Two questions worry your students. One asks them to renounce their loyalty to the Japanese emperor.

"Our parents are not American citizens. If they renounce, what will happen if they are sent back to Japan after the war?"

"The other question asks if we are willing to fight in the U.S. military," another student says. "Why should we fight for a country that keeps us in prisons? But what will happen if we say no?"

"What would you do?" one girl asks.

➻ *To suggest a protest, go to page* **93**.

➻ *To tell the girl she has to make her own decision, turn to page* **94**.

"Maybe you could hold a protest," you suggest. "I'll help, but we'll need to keep it peaceful."

On the day of the protest, you march with the students to the administration building. Mr. Johnston comes out to listen.

Your students explain their concerns about the questionnaire. You are proud of how they speak their minds without making threats.

When they finish, Mr. Johnston replies. "This questionnaire comes from the military and the WRA. I advise that you answer yes to the questions and allow yourselves to be drafted."

The students walk away, frustrated. "What should we do now?" they ask you.

Turn the page.

"It's not really my place to tell you what to do or how to answer," you say. "I don't know what will happen any more than you do. My advice is to follow your hearts."

Some of your students decide to answer no. In a few weeks, you learn that the WRA wants to segregate the camps based on people's responses. Everybody who answered no is sent to the Tule Lake camp in California. You wave good-bye to them and wonder what will become of them in that camp.

Over the next few months, you hear about beatings and other violence at Tule Lake. Some protesters are being sent to prison. You can only hope that your former students are safe.

At Rohwer, classes continue as if nothing had happened. Each morning, you walk to your classroom among groups of students. The girls wear skirts, bobby socks, and saddle shoes. The boys wear crisp pleated pants and white button-down shirts. They look like any other American teenagers.

High school students rushed from one building to another between classes.

Turn the page.

In spring, you hold a graduation ceremony for your class. Most of your students want to do whatever they can to get out of the camp. Some of them take jobs picking fruit in nearby states. Others begin to apply to colleges. When the army announces plans for an all-Japanese unit, some of the boys sign up.

In the summer, you have a one-month break. During that time, you organize extra classes and activities for the internees. Miss Jamison, the art teacher, asks you to help with her art class. Or you think it might be fun to take a group of girls to Camp Shelby in Mississippi. The army camp is hosting a dance for the Japanese soldiers living there.

➻ *To take the girls to the dance, go to page **97**.*

➻ *To help with the art class, turn to page **99**.*

The girls have been looking forward to the dance for weeks. On a Friday afternoon, you and the girls board a local bus that will take you to the camp. But the girls are confused by a sign that says, "Coloreds must sit in back."

In your town and throughout the South, white people and black people are kept separate. There are separate drinking fountains, restrooms, and schools for blacks and whites. You don't really think about it. Segregation is just a way of life.

"Where should we sit?" they ask you. "We're not white, but we're not black, either."

The bus driver answers their question. "You gals can sit in the front. The back is for Negroes only."

Turn the page.

Young women from Rohwer were invited to dances at Camp Shelby.

Once at Camp Shelby, the girls enjoy dancing with the soldiers. Soon, the young men will be sent to fight on the battlefields of France, Italy, and Germany. You know that many of them will die fighting for the country that had once locked them up.

THE END

To follow another path, turn to page 11.
To read the conclusion, turn to page 101.

To follow another path, turn to page 11.
To read the conclusion, turn to page 101.

"I'll be glad to help you, Miss Jamison," you say.

Miss Jamison holds out her hand. "My name's Mabel, but my friends call me Jamie."

Jamie is a wonderful art teacher. She encourages the internees to express themselves through painting, drawing, or sculpture.

You and Jamie teach at Rohwer until it closes on November 30, 1945. For years, you stay in close touch with many of your students.

"You helped make camp brighter during a very bad time in my life," a former student writes several years later. "I will never forget you."

THE END

To follow another path, turn to page 11.
To read the conclusion, turn to page 101.

More than half of the Japanese Americans in the internment camps were children.

CHAPTER 5

Freedom

Over the course of the war, about 120,000 Japanese Americans were forced to live at internment camps across the country. The 10 camps were Granada, Colorado; Gila River, Arizona; Heart Mountain, Wyoming; Jerome, Arkansas; Manzanar, California; Minidoka, Idaho; Poston, Arizona; Rohwer, Arkansas; Topaz, Utah; and Tule Lake, California.

Most of the camps closed at the end of World War II. The last camp to close was Tule Lake in March 1946.

The U.S. government argued that the Japanese Americans were a threat to national security. In addition, about 11,000 German Americans were sent to U.S. internment camps during World War II. Roughly 250 Italian Americans were also interned.

In fact, some of these groups were threats to national security. Between 1938 and 1945, 64 U.S. citizens were convicted of spying and treason. However, none of these people were Japanese.

Still, Japanese Americans faced the most discrimination. Germans and Italians blended in with other white people in the United States. The Japanese were easier to single out. Also, it was Japan, not Germany or Italy, that attacked the United States at Pearl Harbor.

When the camps closed, some internees
moved to Japan. Others returned to where
they had lived before the war started.
And some decided to start a new life in
the Midwest or on the East Coast. There,
they hoped communities would be more
welcoming to Japanese Americans.

Some whites did not welcome the
Japanese Americans back to their
communities after the war.

After the war, many Americans still distrusted the Japanese living among them. Some internees were refused service in places like gas stations and restaurants. Rocks were thrown through windows of some Japanese American homes. Other internees faced discrimination when trying to get jobs or rent apartments or houses.

Many former internees chose not to talk about their lives in the camps. Living in the camps was a humiliating experience, from lack of privacy to being considered enemies.

But some did not stay quiet. They were upset that they had lost their homes and businesses. Many thought the government should pay them money for their losses.

It took many years, but finally, government officials agreed to give money to former internees. Starting in 1990, each internee still living received $20,000. Along with the money, each former internee received an official apology from the government. After 45 years, they finally heard the words, "We're sorry for what the government did to you."

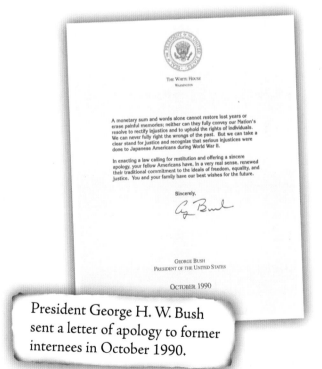

President George H. W. Bush sent a letter of apology to former internees in October 1990.

Time Line

September 1939 — World War II begins.

December 7, 1941 — Japan bombs Pearl Harbor, Hawaii. More than 2,300 U.S. servicemen are killed.

December 8, 1941 — The United States declares war on Japan.

February 19, 1942 — U.S. President Franklin D. Roosevelt signs Executive Order 9066, which requires the removal of all persons of Japanese ancestry living on the West Coast to War Relocation Authority (WRA) camps.

October 30, 1942 — All Japanese people have been removed from their homes on the West Coast.

February 1943 — A loyalty questionnaire is given to all internees age 17 or older in WRA camps.

November 4, 1943–January 14, 1944 — Martial law declared at Tule Lake.

July 1, 1944 — President Roosevelt signs Public Law 405, allowing internees to give up their American citizenship.

December 18, 1944 — The U.S. Supreme Court rules that the United States cannot hold loyal citizens against their will.

August 6, 1945 — The United States drops an atomic bomb on Hiroshima, Japan.

August 9, 1945 — The United States drops an atomic bomb on Nagasaki, Japan.

September 2, 1945 — Japan formally surrenders.

September 4, 1945 — Public Proclamation Number 24 effectively ends Executive Order 9066, paving the way for internees to leave WRA camps.

March 20, 1946 — Tule Lake is the last WRA camp to close.

September 1971 — Japanese Americans who gave up their U.S. citizenship in the camps have their rights restored.

August 10, 1988 — U.S. President Ronald Reagan signs a law providing for an official apology and $20,000 in payments to each former internee.

October 9, 1990 — The first nine payments are made at a formal ceremony.

OTHER PATHS TO EXPLORE

In this book, you've seen how the internment of Japanese Americans during World War II was experienced from three points of view.

Perspectives on history are as varied as the people who lived it. You can explore other paths on your own to learn more about what happened. Seeing history from many points of view is an important part of understanding it.

Here are some ideas for other Japanese American internment points of view to explore:

+ The decision to move all Japanese Americans to internment camps was not an easy one. If you were a government official in 1942, how would you have felt?

+ Soldiers helped round up Japanese Americans for evacuation and guarded the camps to prevent internees from escaping. What was it like to be a soldier assigned to guarding the camps?

+ In addition to the Japanese Americans, many German Americans and Italian Americans were moved to WRA camps. How did their experiences differ from those of the Japanese?

READ MORE

Burgan, Michael. *The Japanese American Internment: Civil Liberties Denied.* Minneapolis: Compass Point Books, 2007.

Cooper, Michael L. *Remembering Manzanar: Life in a Japanese Relocation Camp.* New York: Clarion Books, 2002.

Donlan, Leni. *How Did This Happen Here?: Japanese Internment Camps.* Chicago: Raintree, 2008.

Kent, Deborah. *The Tragic History of the Japanese-American Internment Camps.* Berkeley Heights, N.J.: Enslow, 2007.

INTERNET SITES

FactHound offers a safe, fun way to find Internet sites related to this book. All of the sites on FactHound have been researched by our staff.

109

Here's how:

1. Visit *www.facthound.com*
2. Choose your grade level.
3. Type in this book ID **1429613580** for age-appropriate sites. You may also browse subjects by clicking on letters, or by clicking on pictures and words.
4. Click on the **Fetch It** button.

FactHound will fetch the best sites for you!

GLOSSARY

allegiance (uh-LEE-junss) — loyal support for someone or something, such as a country

barracks (BEAR-uhks) — buildings often used to house soldiers

battalion (buh-TAL-yuhn) — a large unit of soldiers

evacuation (i-vak-yoo-AY-shuhn) — the removal of large numbers of people from an area

infamy (IN-fuh-mee) — a lasting, widespread, and deep-rooted evil reputation brought about by something criminal, shocking, or brutal

internee (in-tuhr-NEE) — a person who is forced to live at an internment camp

110

martial law (MAR-shuhl LAW) — rule by the army in time of war or emergency

renounce (ruh-NOUNSS) — to give up or take back

resistance (ri-ZISS-tuhnss) — fighting back

riot (RYE-uht) — a violent and often uncontrollable gathering of people

segregate (SEG-ruh-gate) — to separate or keep people or things apart from the main group

BIBLIOGRAPHY

Austin, Allan W. *From Concentration Camp to Campus: Japanese American Students and World War II.* Urbana, Ill.: University of Illinois Press, 2004.

Fugita, Stephen S. and Marilyn Fernandez. *Altered Lives, Enduring Community: Japanese Americans Remember Their World War II Incarceration.* Seattle: University of Washington Press, 2004.

James, Thomas. "The Education of Japanese Americans at Tule Lake, 1942–1946." *Pacific Historical Review* 56, no. 1 (February 1987): 25–58.

Manzanar National Historic Site
http://www.nps.gov/manz/

Matsumoto, Valerie. "Japanese American Women during World War II." *Frontiers: A Journal of Women Studies* 8, no. 1 (1984): 6–14.

Murray, Alice Yang, ed. *What Did the Internment of Japanese Americans Mean?* Boston: Bedford/St. Martin's, 2000.

Tateishi, John, ed. *And Justice for All: An Oral History of the Japanese American Detention Camps.* Seattle: University of Washington Press, 1999.

111

INDEX